CLASSIC CARS
★ AN IMAGINATION LIBRARY SERIES ★

THE STORY OF

Volkswagen
Beetles

by David K. Wright

Gareth Stevens Publishing
A WORLD ALMANAC EDUCATION GROUP COMPANY

Please visit our web site at: www.garethstevens.com
For a free color catalog describing Gareth Stevens Publishing's
list of high-quality books and multimedia programs,
call 1-800-542-2595 (USA) or 1-800-387-3178 (Canada).
Gareth Stevens Publishing's fax: (414) 332-3567.

Library of Congress Cataloging-in-Publication Data

Wright, David K.
    The story of Volkswagen Beetles / by David K. Wright.
        p. cm. — (Classic cars: an imagination library series)
    Includes bibliographical references and index.
    Summary: Surveys the history of the car known as the Volkswagen Beetle,
describing how its popularity endured despite the fact that it was not sold in
the United States between 1981 and 1998.
    ISBN 0-8368-3194-2 (lib. bdg.)
    1. Volkswagen automobile—History—Juvenile literature. 2. Volkswagen
Beetle automobile—History—Juvenile literature. [1. Volkswagen Beetle
automobile—History.] I. Title.
TL215.V6W75   2002
629.222'2—dc21   2002021180

First published in 2002 by
Gareth Stevens Publishing
A World Almanac Education Group Company
330 West Olive Street, Suite 100
Milwaukee, WI 53212 USA

Text: David K. Wright
Cover design and page layout: Scott M. Krall
Series editor: Jim Mezzanotte
Picture Researcher: Diane Laska-Swanke

Photo credits: Cover, pp. 5, 11, 13 © Ron Kimball; p. 7 © The Mariner's Museum/CORBIS;
p. 9 © Richard Adams; pp. 15, 17 © Isaac Hernández/MercuryPress.com; p. 19 © Bettmann/CORBIS;
p. 21 Courtesy of Susan Ashley and Diane Laska-Swanke

Printed in the United States of America

1 2 3 4 5 6 7 8 9 06 05 04 03 02

Front cover: **This 1950 Volkswagen Beetle
has its engine in the rear. The Beetle's round
shape did not change much over the years!**

TABLE OF CONTENTS

Words that appear in the glossary are printed in **boldface** type the first time they occur in the text.

THE BEETLE IS BORN

The year was 1935. Germany needed a car that everybody could buy. A German **engineer** named Ferdinand Porsche created the best design. His car was called the *Volkswagen*, which means "people's car" in German. Many years later, Porsche made his own famous sports cars.

The Volkswagen was an unusual car. It was small and round, and its engine was in the back, where most cars had trunks. The engine was cooled by air, so it did not need a **radiator**. The headlights looked like two big eyes. Some people thought the car looked like a bug — like a **beetle**!

This Volkswagen is a 1949 convertible model.
Many early buyers of Volkswagens thought
the small, round cars looked like beetles.

BEETLES EVERYWHERE

In 1939, World War II began. Plans for making the Beetle were put on hold. The war ended in 1945. After the war, Volkswagen started making the Beetle. The small, cheap car soon became popular. It could be seen all over Europe — and beyond.

Volkswagen Beetles were first **imported** into the United States in 1949. Advertisements for the Beetle made fun of the way it looked. The Beetle was different from most cars made in the United States. But many people liked this new car, and they bought it.

Volkswagens from Germany arrive in Baltimore in 1956. They were very different from most cars made in the United States at the time.

FUN WITH THE BUG

Volkswagen Beetles were slow cars. They also had tiny **interiors**, especially compared to the big, roomy cars made in the United States. The driver and the front-seat passenger sat very close to the windshield.

Beetles had their faults, but most Beetle owners loved their "Bugs." One owner drove his Beetle into a river and discovered it could float!

Other owners **modified** their Beetles. Owners in California replaced the buglike bodies with special bodies made of **fiberglass** and then added fat tires. The dune buggy was born!

People had fun with Volkswagens! The person who built this 1965 dune buggy replaced the Beetle body with a lightweight fiberglass body.

VOLKSWAGENS ON PARADE

After a while, people of all ages were riding around in Volkswagens — parents, children, even grandmas and grandpas. Volkswagen, or "VW" for short, had become a familiar name to many people.

In the 1960s and early 1970s, VWs were very popular with young people in the United States. They often drove VW Beetles off to college.

During this time, the Beetle and its van cousin, the VW Microbus, often became rolling art projects. Young people decorated their VWs with big vinyl daisies, bumper stickers, and crazy paint jobs. These VWs attracted a lot of attention!

In the 1960s and 1970s, some people added crazy decorations to their Volkswagen Beetles. This 1969 model is covered with marble and stained glass.

HERBIE, THE LOVE BUG

In 1969, a new kind of star was born. That year, Walt Disney Studios released a movie called *The Love Bug*. A VW Bug named Herbie starred in the movie.

Herbie is a Volkswagen with a mind of its own. This special Bug laughs, "winks" its headlights, and performs impossible stunts. Herbie helps Jim, a race car driver. Together, they win races.

Many children went to see *The Love Bug*, and they had fun watching Herbie. Because of the movie, the Volkswagen Beetle became popular with a new **generation** of people. Herbie starred in more movies. This Bug had become a big hit!

Say hello to Herbie, the "Love Bug," star of the 1969 Disney film of the same name. This Volkswagen Beetle is actually a 1963 model.

BETTER BEETLES

The Beetle was not like most cars — year after year, its basic shape stayed the same. Volkswagen did change the Beetle, however, making many improvements to the car.

Over the years, the Beetle's engine became larger, so it produced more **horsepower**. The car's brakes were also improved, so it stopped quicker. Inside, the seats became bigger and more comfortable, and more room was created for back-seat passengers.

In the 1970s, Volkswagen made the "Super Beetle." It had a more powerful engine, more space in the trunk, and larger fenders and taillights.

The Super Beetles that Volkswagen made in the 1970s were faster and roomier than earlier Beetles, but they did not look too different!

THE BEETLE LIVES ON

By 1972, Volkswagen had made more than fifteen million Beetles. By then, however, other carmakers in Europe, the United States, and Japan were also building small cars that people enjoyed driving.

Volkswagen sold fewer and fewer Beetles. The company made plans to build new kinds of cars. In 1980, Volkswagen sold its last Beetle in the United States. The company no longer made the Beetle at its German factories.

But the Beetle was still being made at factories in other countries, such as Brazil and Mexico. In 1981, a Mexican factory built the twenty millionth Beetle. Today, Beetles are still made in Mexico. The Beetle lives on!

Volkswagen Beetles roam the streets of a city in Mexico, where the Beetle is still made. Some people in Mexico use Beetles as taxis!

RACING BEETLES

In the 1960s, some people began making race cars from parts of Volkswagen Beetles. With so many Beetles in the world, parts for the cars were cheap and easy to find.

These race cars were called Formula Vees. The cars used the Beetle's engine, **transmission**, and **suspension**. They had sleek, tubelike bodies with no fenders over the wheels. Their bodies were made of fiberglass and lightweight metal.

People still race Formula Vees today. The fastest Formula Vees can reach speeds of up to 160 miles (250 kilometers) per hour!

These Formula Vees are beginning a race in Florida in 1968. A Formula Vee uses many parts from a Beetle, but it is definitely a race car!

A BRAND NEW BEETLE

In 1998, almost twenty years after Volkswagen stopped selling Beetles in the United States, the company introduced an entirely new version of the Beetle. The Beetle was reborn!

The new Beetle has its engine in the front, instead of in the back. Unlike the old Beetle, it also has **front-wheel drive**. The new Beetle has many modern **innovations**, and it is just as fast as most other cars today. But it still looks like a Beetle.

This new Beetle has sold very well in the United States and other countries. It should be around for many years to come!

The new Beetle looks a lot like the old Beetle, but it is actually very different! It has front-wheel drive and a roomier interior, and it is much faster.

MORE TO READ AND VIEW

Books (Nonfiction)　*All Aboard Cars.* Catherine Daly-Weir (Grosset & Dunlap)
Beetlemania: The Story of the Car that Captured the Hearts of Millions. Kate McLeod (Smithmark Publishing)
Big Book of Cars. Trevor Lord (DK Publishing)
Cars. Investigations (series). Peter Harrison (Lorenz Books)
The Volkswagen Beetle. Linda Jean Lally (Capstone Press)

Books (Fiction)　*The Beetle and Me: A Love Story.* Karen Romano Young (Greenwillow)
The Love Bug. The Wonderful World of Disney (series). Scott Sorrentino (Disney Press)

Videos (Nonfiction)　*A&E Top 10: Cars That Changed the Automobile Industry.* (A&E)
History of the Volkswagen. (White Star)
The Visual History of Cars: Volkswagen. (MPI Home Video)

Videos (Fiction)　*Herbie Goes to Monte Carlo.* (Disney Studios)
Herbie Rides Again. (Disney Studios)
The Love Bug. (Disney Studios)

PLACES TO WRITE AND VISIT

Here are two places to contact for more information:

Auto World Car Museum
Business Route 54
Fulton, MO 65251
USA
1-573-642-2080

National Automobile Museum
10 Lake Street South
Reno, NV 89501
USA
1-775-333-9300
www.automuseum.org/info.html

WEB SITES

Web sites change frequently, but we believe the following web sites are going to last. You can also use good search engines, such as **Yahooligans!** [www.yahooligans.com] or **Google** [www.google.com], to find more information about Volkswagen Beetles. Here are some keywords to help you: *dune buggy, Formula Vee, people's car, Porsche, Volkswagen, VW Beetle,* and *VW Bug.*

www4.tpgi.com.au/users/kstrong/
Beetle Cars & Kombi Vans for Kids is a web site from Australia. It has a lot of interesting information about Volkswagen Beetles and Microbuses, and it has many pictures, too. In Australia, some people call VW Microbuses kombi vans!

www.bugtales.com/gallery.htm
This web site has a page called *The Picture Gallery*. It has many old and new pictures of Volkswagen Beetles.

www.geocities.com/dhtlbl
Visit *Herbie the Love Bug's Garage* for a lot of information about Herbie!

www.geocities.com/isawyou/ vw_pictures.html
VW Beetle Photo Gallery has a lot of pictures of Volkswagen Beetles!

www.geocities.com/MotorCity/Speedway/ 1367/beetle.html
Tom's Beetle restoration site tells all about fixing a 1966 Volkswagen Beetle so it seems like it is brand new.

www.virtualbeetlemuseum.com
Who says a museum cannot be on the Internet? This web site shows views of the Beetle and other Volkswagens, from all different angles.

www.vwbeetle.org/netscape-gall.php
This web site also has many interesting pictures of Volkswagen Beetles.

www.vw.com/newbeetle/index.html
Visit this site to see pictures of the new Beetle.

GLOSSARY

You can find these words on the pages listed. Reading a word in a sentence helps you understand it even better.

beetle (BEAT-uhl) — a round insect that has hard front wings for protection 4

engineer (ehn-jin-EAR) — a person who plans the construction of structures or machines, such as cars 4

fiberglass (FYE-ber-glas) — a material made of thin glass threads and plastic that can be molded into different shapes 8, 18

front-wheel drive (FRUHNT-weel DRYV) — a system for making a car go that uses the engine to turn the front wheels 20

generation (jen-er-RAY-shun) — a group of people who are about the same age 12

horsepower (HORS-pow-ur) — the unit of measurement for an engine's power 14

imported (im-PORT-ed) — brought in from another country 6

innovations (in-oh-VAY-shunz) — new inventions or ways of doing things 20

interiors (in-TEAR-e-urz) — the inside spaces of things, such as houses or cars 8, 20

modified (MOD-if-eyed) — made changes to something 8

radiator (RAY-dee-ay-tor) — the part of a car that cools a special liquid flowing through the engine to keep the engine from getting too hot 4

suspension (suh-SPEN-shun) — the system that connects wheels to the rest of a car, and keeps a car steady over bumps 18

transmission (tranz-MISH-shun) — the part of a car that holds many gears for sending power from the engine to the wheels 18

INDEX